*Flowers
of
Greece*

FLOWERS
of
GREECE

by George Sfikas

EFSTATHIADIS GROUP

EFSTATHIADIS GROUP S.A.
14, Valtetsiou Str.
106 80 Athens
Tel: (01) 5254650, 6450113
Fax: (01) 5254657
GREECE

ISBN 960 226 197 8

© **Efstathiadis Group A.E. 1998**

Printed and bound in Greece

Contents

Endemic to Crete, this rare plant grows in mountain meadows. It is one of the loveliest of the species Tulipa to be found in Greece. Flowers April-May.

Seltene endemische Pflanze der Insel Kreta, wo sie auf den gebirgigen Wiesen zu finden ist. Eine der schönsten Sorten von Tulpen, die es in Griechenland gibt. Sie blüht im April-Mai.

Pianta rara endemica dell'isola di Creta ove spunta nei prati montuosi. E'una delle più belle specie di tulipano esistenti in Grecia. Fiorisce in aprile-maggio.

Plante rare endémique de l'île de Crète où elle pousse dans les prairies des montagnes. C'est une des meilleures espèces de tulipe qui existent en Grèce. Elle fleurit en avril-mai.

Φυτό σπάνιο ἐνδημικό τῆς νήσου Κρήτης ὅπου φυτρώνει στά ὀρεινά λειβάδια. Εἶναι ἕνα ἀπό τά ὡραιότερα εἴδη τουλίπας πού ὑπάρχουν στόν ἑλληνικό χῶρο. Ἀνθίζει τόν Ἀπρίλιο-Μάϊο.

Sällsynt planta, inhemsk på Kreta, där den växer på bergsängarna. Det är en av de vackraste sorterna tulpaner, som finns i Grekland. Den blommar under april-maj.

Een zeldzame plant, die inheems is op het eiland Kreta, waar hij op de bergweiden groeit. Een van de mooiste in Griekenland voorkomende soorten tulpen. Bloeitijd april-mei.

クレタ島特有の花で山間の草地に見られる。 ギリシャに咲く同品種の花々のうちで最も美しいもののひとつ。 開花期4～5月.

1. **TULIPA SAXATILIS** *SIEB.*

This species is widely distributed in alpine zone areas throughout the mainland including the Peloponnese. It can be found in alpine regions where it favours stony places. Flowers May-July.

Diese Sorte wächst auf steinernem Boden der hochen Zone der griechischen Berge. Es ist ziemlich verbreitet auf allen grossen Bergen des griechischen Festlandes und auf dem Peloponnes. Blüht im Mai-Juli.

Questa specie spunta in luoghi pietrosi delle zone alpine delle montagne greche. E'molto diffusa su per le grandi montagne della Grecia continentale e del Peloponneso. Fiorisce in maggio-luglio.

Cette espèce pousse dans les lieux pierreux de la zone alpine des montagnes grecques. Elle est très répandue dans toutes les grandes montagnes de la Grèce continentale et du Péloponnèse. Elle fleurit en mai-juillet.

Τό εἶδος αὐτό φυτρώνει σέ πετρώδεις τοποθεσίες τῆς ἀλπικῆς ζώνης τῶν ἑλληνικῶν βουνῶν. Εἶναι ἀρκετά διαδεδομένο σέ ὅλα τά μεγάλα βουνά τῆς Ἡπειρωτικῆς Ἑλλάδος καί τῆς Πελοποννήσου. Ἀνθίζει τόν Μάϊο-Ἰούλιο.

Denna sort växer på steniga platser i fjällzonen i de grekiska bergen. Den är tämligen utbredd på alla de stora bergen på grekiska fastlandet och på Peloponnisos. Blommar i maj-juli.

Deze ranonkelsoort groet op steenachtige plaatsen in de hoge gedeelten van het Griekse bergland, en komt wijd verspreid voor op alle hoge bergen op het Griekse vasteland (Epirus) en op de Peloponnesus. Bloeitijd mei-juli.

ペロポネソスを含むギリシャ本土の山々に広く見られる。　特に高山の岩肌に見られることが多い。　開花期 5～6月.

2 **RANUNCULUS BREVIFOLIUS** *TEN.*

Crocus sieberi is indigenous to southern Greece, the Peloponnese and Crete. The variety, Crocus atticus, grows in the mountains of southern Greece. Flowers April-May.

Crocus Sieberi ist eine endemische Pflanze aus Südgriechenland, aus dem Peloponnes und aus Kreta. Seine verwandte Sorte, Atticus, lebt auf den Bergen Südgriechenlands. Blüht im April-Mai.

Il Crocus Sieberi è una pianta endemica del sud delle Grecia, del Peloponneso e dell'isola di Creta. La sua varietà Atticus prospera su per le montagne delle Grecia meridionale. Fiorisce in aprile-maggio.

La Crocus Sieberi est une plante endémique du sud de la Grèce, du Péloponnèse et de l'île de Crète. Sa variété Atticus vit dans les montagnes de la Grèce du sud. Elle fleurit en avril-mai.

Ὁ crocus sieberi εἶναι ἕνα εἶδος ἐνδημικό τῆς Ν. Ἑλλάδος, τῆς Πελοποννήσου καί τῆς Κρήτης. Ἡ ποικιλία του Atticus ζῆ στά βουνά τῆς Ν. Ἑλλάδος. Ἀνθίζει τόν Ἀπρίλιο-Μάϊο.

Krokus sieberi är en inhemsk sort från södra Grekland, Peloponnisos och Kreta. En annan liknande art Atticus finns på bergen i södra Grekland. Blommar i april-maj.

De Crocus Sieberi is inheems in Zuid-Griekenland, op de Peloponnesus en op Kreta. Zijn variëteit Crocus Atticus groeit in de bergen van Noord-Griekenland. Bloeitijd april-mei.

南ギリシャ、ペロポネソス、クレタ島に見られるが、中でも特に南ギリシャの山々に種類が多い。 開花期4〜5月。

3   **CROCUS SIEBERI** *J. GAY.*
VAR. ATTICUS *BOISS & ORPH.*

This exquisite, wonderfully scented plant, known popularly as the Madonna lily, is cultivated throughout Greece. It is now rarely found growing in the wild. Prefers steep, sub-alpine slopes. Flowers April-June.

Diese wunderschöne Pflanze mit dem einmaligen Duft, die unter dem Namen «Jungfräuliche Lilie» bekannt ist, wird in ganz Griechenland aufgezogen. Als Wildpflanze trifft man sie heute an abschüssigen Orten mittleren Höhenmessers. Sie blüht im April-Juni.

Questa bella pianta dall'aroma meraviglioso, conosciuta sotto la denominazione di «giglio vergine» viene coltivata dappertutto in Grecia. Raramente s'incontra nella sua forma selvatica su per le scarpate di media altitudine.

Cette plante si belle à l'arôme merveilleux, qui est connue sous le nom de «lis vierge», se cultive partout en Grèce. On peut la rencontrer rarement sous sa forme sauvage dans les lieux escarpés d'altitude moyenne. Elle fleurit en avril-juin.

Τό ὡραιότατο αὐτό φυτό μέ τό θαυμάσιο ἄρωμα πού εἶναι γνωστό σάν «Παρθενικός κρίνος» καλλιεργεῖται σ' ὅλη τήν Ἑλλάδα. Σέ αὐτοφυή μορφή ἀπαντᾶται σήμερα σέ ἐλάχιστες ἀπόκρημνες τοποθεσίες μέσου ὑψομέτρου. Ἀνθίζει τόν Ἀπρίλιο-Ἰούνιο.

Denna underbara växt med den utsökta doften, som är känd som Jungfrulilja, odlas i hela Grekland. I vilt tillstånd finner man den ytterst sällan och då på branta platser på medelhöjd. Blommar i april-juni.

Deze prachtige plant met zijn heerlijke geur, die bekend is onder de naam "maagdenlelie", wordt overal in Griekenland gekweekt, en komt nog maar zelden in het wild voor op steile hellingen op matige hoogten. Bloeitijd april-juni.

素晴しい香をもつこの花は「マドンナの百合」として知られ、ギリシャ全土で栽培されており、今日では野生のものは なかなか見られない。 山あいの斜面を好む。 開花期4～6月.

4. LILIUM CANDIDUM *L.*

This plant is common at sub-alpine levels where it establishes itself in rock fissures and adorns the rocks with brilliant clusters of blooms. Flowers April-June.

Gewöhnliche Pflanze der griechischen Berge, wo wir sie an Stellen mittleren Höhenmessers treffen. Wächst in den Spaltungen der Felsen, die sie mit ihren wunderschönen Blumensträusschen schmückt. Sie blüht im April-Juni.

E'una pianta comune delle montagne greche che cresce nelle zone di media altitudine. Spunta nei crepacci delle rocce che vengono adornate da meravigliosi mazzi di fiori. Fiorisce in aprile-giugno.

C'est une plante commune aux montagnes grecques qui crôt dans les lieux d'altitude moyenne. Elle pousse dans les crevasses des rochers les garnissant avec ses merveilleux bouquets de fleurs. Elle fleurit en avril-juin.

Κοινό φυτό τῶν ἑλληνικῶν βουνῶν ὅπου τό συναντοῦμε σέ τοποθεσίες μέσου ὕψους. Φυτρώνει μέσα στίς σχισμές τῶν βράχων πού τούς στολίζει μέ τά θαυμάσια μπουκέτα τῶν λουλουδιῶν του. 'Ανθίζει τόν 'Απρίλιο-'Ιούνιο.

En vanlig växt i de grekiska bergen, där man möter den på medelhöjd. Den skjuter upp i sprickor i klippor, som pryds med underbara buketter av denna blomma. Blommar i april-juni.

Een zeer algemene plant van de Griekse bergen, waar hij op matige hoogte groeit in scheuren in de rotsen, die hij opluisterd met zijn prachtige bloemboeketten. Bloeitijd april-juni.

中高地の岩の害れ目に群生し、岩肌を美しく飾る。　開花期 4〜6月.

5. **AUBRIETIA DELTOIDEA** *D.C.*

This charming rock dweller appears on the mountains of southern Greece as soon as the hot, dry Greek summer has passed. Flowers September-October.

Diese hübsche kleine Lilie wächst auf den Felsen der Berge Südgriechenlands, nachdem der heisse und trockene griechische Sommer vorbei ist. Sie blüht im September-Oktober.

Questo bello e piccolo giglio spunta sulle rocce montuose della Grecia meridionale, non appena la calura e la temperatura secca dell'estate greca spariscono. Fiorisce in settembre-ottobre.

Ce beau petit lis pousse sur les rochers des montagnes grecques dans le sud du pays. Dès que l'été chaud et sec de la Grèce nous quitte, il fait son apparition. Il donne ses fleurs en septembre-octobre.

Τό ὄμορφο αὐτό κρινάκι θγαίνει στά θράχια τῶν θουνῶν τῆς Ν. Ἑλλάδος μόλις περάσει τό ζεστό καί ξηρό ἑλληνικό καλοκαίρι. Ἀνθίζει τόν Σεπτέμβριο- Ὀκτώβριο.

Denna vackra lilja växer bland klippor i bergen i södra Grekland, så snart den varma och torra grekiska sommaren är över. Blommar i september-oktober.

Deze fraaie kleine lelie groeit op rotsen in de bergen in Zuid-Griekenland zodra de warme droge Griekse zomer voorbij is. Bloeitijd september-oktober.

暑く乾いたギリシャの夏が過ぎる頃に、南部ギリシャの山々の岩面にチャーミングな姿を見せる。　開花期 9〜10月.

6. **STERNBERGIA LUTEA** *KER.*

Many species of the genus Fritillaria are found in Greece. It resembles the tulip but, unlike the tulip, has drooping flowers and is generally less brightly coloured. The species illustrated is found in mainland Greece and flowers from April to May.

Viele Arten der Gattung Fritillaria leben in Griechenland. Sie sehen aus wie Tulpen, doch ihre Blüten hängen nach unten und ihre Farben sind nicht so stark. Die Sorte auf dem Bild lebt auf dem Festland in Griechenland und blüht im April-Mai.

Sono numerose le specie del genere Fritillaria esistenti in Grecia. Somigliano ai tulipani però i loro fiori pendono verso il basso ed i loro colori sono meno vivi. Il genere illustrato a fianco prospera nella Grecia continentale e fiorisce in aprile-maggio.

Plusieurs espèces du genre Fritillaria existent en Grèce. Elles ressemblent aux tulipes mais leurs fleurs penchent vers le bas et leurs couleurs sont moins vives. Le genre présenté par notre image se trouve dans la Grèce continentale et fleurit en avril-mai.

Πολλά εἴδη τοῦ γένους Fritillaria ζοῦν στόν ἑλληνικό χῶρο. Μοιάζουν μέ τουλίπες ἀλλά τά ἄνθη τους γέρνουν πρός τά κάτω καί ἔχουν χρώματα λιγώτερο ἔντονα. Τό εἶδος πού βλέπετε στήν εἰκόνα ζῆ στήν ἠπειρωτική Ἑλλάδα καί ἀνθίζει τόν Ἀπρίλιο-Μάιο.

Många sorter av familjen Fritillaria finns det i Grekland. Den ser ut som en tulpan, men blommorna lutar nedåt, och har inte så skarpa färger. Sorten vi ser på fotografiet finns på grekiska fastlandet och blommar i april-maj.

Vele soorten van het geslacht Fritillaria komen in Griekenland voor. Zij lijken op tulpen, maar zij hebben, anders dan tulpen, naar beneden gerichte bloemen en als regel minder levendige kleuren. De hier afgebeelde soort groeit op het vasteland van Griekenland en bloeit in april-mei.

この花の仲間はギリシャでは多種見つけることができる。チューリップに似ているが、チューリップとちがって花は地面に向かって垂れ下がっており。色もチューリップのような明るい色ではない。 写真の花はギリシャ本土に見られるもので、開花期は4～5月。

7. **FRITILLARIA GRAECA** *BOISS. & SPRUN.*

This rare plant grows at high altitudes in meadows and rocky places on the mountains of northern Greece. Flowers June-August.

Seltene Pflanze der Berge Nordgriechenlands, wo sie auf Wiesen und Felsen grossen Höhenmessers lebt. Sie blüht im Juni-August.

Pianta rara delle montagne della Grecia settentrionale ove spunta sulle rocce e nei prati di grande altitudine. Fiorisce in giugno-agosto.

Plante rare des montagnes de la Grèce du nord où elle pousse sur les rochers et aux prairies de grande altitude. Elle fleurit en juin-août.

Σπάνιο φυτό τῶν βουνῶν τῆς Β. ῾Ελλάδος ὅπου ζῇ στά λιβάδια καί στούς βράχους μεγάλου ὑψομέτρου. ᾿Ανθίζει τόν ᾿Ιούνιο-Αὔγουστο.

En sällsynt planta ifrån bergen i norra Grekland, där den växer på ängarna och bland klipporna på hög höjd. Blommar i juni-augusti.

Een zeldzame plant van de bergen van Noord-Griekenland, waar hij op grote hoogte in weiden en op rotsen groeit. Bloeitijd juni-augustus.

高地の草地や北部ギリシャの山々に咲く珍しい花. 開花期6~8月.

8. **GERANIUM SUBCAULESCENS** *L. HER.*

This small member of the lily family grows in bushy places at low altitudes in southern Greece and the Peloponnese. It blooms late in the autumn in lonely splendour, most other plants in the area having blossomed earlier in the season.

Diese kleine Lilie lebt an buschigen Stellen niedrigen Höhenmessers in Südgriechenland und auf dem Peloponnes. Sie blüht spät im Herbst, d.h. in einer Jahreszeit, in der es sehr wenige Pflanzen in diesen Gegenden gibt.

Questo piccolo giglio cresce nei campi cespugliosi di bassa altitudine della Grecia meridonale e del Peloponneso. Fiorisce nel tardo autunno, ossia in una stagione in cui pochissimi sono i fiori esistenti in queste regioni.

Ce petit lis cröt dans les champs buissonneux de basse altitude de la Grèce du sud et du Péloponnèse. Il donne ses fleurs tard en automne, soit à une époque á laquelle très peu de fleurs existent dans ces lieux.

Τό μικρό αὐτό κρινάκι ζῆ στούς θαμνότοπους χαμηλοῦ ὑψομέτρου τῆς Ν. Ἑλλάδος καί τῆς Πελοποννήσου. Ἀνθίζει ἀργά τό φθινόπωρο, σέ ἐποχή δηλαδή πού πολύ λίγα λουλούδια ὑπάρχουν σ᾽ αὐτά τά μέρη.

Denna lilla lilja växer på platser med buskar på låg höjd i södra Grekland och på Peloponnisos. Blommar sent på hösten, dvs. under en tid, då det finns mycket få blommor på dessa platser.

Deze kleine lelie groeit op met laag struikgewas begroeide plaatsen op geringe hoogte in Zuid-Griekenland en op de Peloponnesus. Hij bloeit laat in de herfst, dus wanneer er in deze streken zeer weinig planten bloeien.

ユリ科に属するこの小さな花は、南ギリシャとペロポネソスの低地のかん木地帯に見られる。 他の花々が一通り咲き終えた晩秋に花開き ひっそりとした香を漂わせる。

9. **MERENDERA ATTICA** *BOISS.*

Five species of Aquilegia, also known as columbine, are found in Greece. The rarest of them is the species illustrated, which grows in the mountains of central Greece and the Peloponnese. Flowers May-July.

Fünf Sorten von Aquilegia sind bekannt auch als Akeleien in Griechenland. Unter diesen ist die Art unseres Bildes die seltenste. Sie lebt auf den Bergen des Peloponnes und Mittelgriechenlands. Sie blüht im Mai-Juli.

Esistono in Grecia cinque specie di Aquilegia, note sotto la denominazione di Colombine. Di queste specie la più rara è quella qui illustrata che cresce su per le montagne del Peloponneso e della Grecia centrale. Fiorisce in giugno-agosto.

Cinq espèces de Aquilegia, connues sous le nom de Colombines, vivent en Grèce. De ces espèces la plus rare est celle de notre image qui pousse sur les montagnes du Péloponnèse et de la Grèce centrale. Elle fleurit en juin-août.

Πέντε είδη ᾽Ακουϊλέγια γνωστά καί σάν Κολομπίνες ζοῦν στήν ᾽Ελλάδα. ᾽Απ᾽ αὐτά τό πιό σπάνιο εἶναι τό εἶδος τῆς εἰκόνας μας πού ζῆ στά βουνά τῆς Πελοποννήσου καί τῆς Κεντρικῆς ᾽Ελλάδος. ᾽Ανθίζει τόν Μάϊο-᾽Ιούλιο.

Fem sorter Aquileja, även kända som Kolombiner, växer det i Grekland. Bland dem är blomman vi ser på fotografiet den mest sällsynta, som växer i bergen på Peloponnisos och i centrala Grekland. Blommar i maj-juli.

Vijf soorten Aquilegia (Akelei), ook bekend als Colombine, zijn bekend in Griekenland. Van deze soorten is de zeldzaamste de hier afgebeelde soort, die in de bergen van de Peloponnesus en van Centraal Griekenland groeit. Bloeitijd mei-juli.

おだまきという名でも知られるこの花の仲間は、ギリシャには5品種ある。 写真はその中でも最も珍しい種類で 中部ギリシャとペロポネソスの山々に見られる。 開花期5〜7月。

10. **AQUILEGIA OTHONIS** *ORPH.*

This plant is commonly found in the mountains throughout Greece, its golden-yellow blossoms glowing among the stark, alpine rocks. Flowers June-August.

Gewöhnliche Pflanze der Berge ganze Griechenlands, wo sie mit ihren goldgelblichen Blüten die kahlen gebirgigen Felsen schmückt. Sie blüht im Juni-August.

Pianta comune che spunta su per le montagne greche. Adorna dei suoi fiori, di colore giallo-aureo, le rocce brulle. Fiorisce in giugno-agosto.

Plante commune aux montagnes grecques. Elle garnit avec ses fleurs, d'une couleur jaune-or, les rochers dénudés. Elle fleurit en juin-août.

Φυτό κοινό στά βουνά όλης τής Ελλάδος όπου στολίζει μέ τά χρυσοκίτρινα άνθη του τούς γυμνούς ορεινούς βράχους. Ανθίζει τόν Ιούνιο-Αύγουστο.

En vanlig växt på bergen i hela Grekland, där den pryder de nakna bergsklipporna med sina guldgula blommor. Blommar i juni-augusti.

Een zeer algemene plant in de bergen overal in Griekenland, waar hij met zijn goudgele bloemen het kale bergland versiert. Bloeitijd juni-augustus.

キリシャ全土の山地で見られる一般的な花。 固い岩の間に黄金色の花びらを広げる。 開花期6〜8月.

11. **LINUM ELEGANS** *SPRUN.*

This species is a small shrub characteristic of the maquis throughout Greece. Its fruit, known locally as "koumara," are not only beautiful but edible. It flowers in the autumn, and its fruit of previous year ripens in autumn too.

Diese Sorte ist ein kleiner Busch sehr gewöhnlich in den Busch-Gegenden ganz Griechenlands. Ihre Früchte, die bekannten Bärentrauben, sind nicht nur schön, sondern auch essbar. Sie blüht im Herbst, und in der selben Jahreszeit werden die Früchte des vorrigen Jahres reif.

Questa specie è un piccolo cespuglio che s'incontra frequentemente in tutte le regioni cespugliose della Grecia. I suoi frutti sono le corbezzole, che oltre alla loro bellezza sono pur commestibili. Fiorisce in autunno e nella stessa stagione maturano i frutti dell'anno precedente.

Cette espèce est un petit buisson que l'on rencontre fréquemment dans toutes les régions buissonneuses de la Grèce. Ses fruits sont les arbouses qui, outre leur beauté, sont aussi mangeables. L'arbousier fleurit en automne et en même temps ses fruits de l'année précédente mûrissent.

Τό εἶδος αὐτό εἶναι ἕνας μικρός θάμνος κοινός στούς θαμνότοπους ὅλης τῆς Ἑλλάδος. Οἱ καρποί του, τά γνωστά κούμαρα, ἐκτός ἀπό τήν ὁμορφιά τους εἶναι καί φαγώσιμοι. Ἀνθίζει τό φθινόπωρο καί τήν ἴδια ἐποχή ὡριμάζουν οἱ καρποί τῆς προηγούμενης χρονιάς.

Detta är en liten vanlig buske i buskvegetationen i hela Grekland. Dess frukter, som kallas koumara, är både vackra och ätbara. Blommar på hösten och under samma tid mognar frukterna från det föregående året.

Deze soort is een lage, ook in de winter groene heester, die overal in Griekenland voorkomt in die streken welke met struikgewas zijn begroeid. De vruchten zijn niet alleen fraai maar ook eetbaar. Hij bloeit in de herfst en tegelijkertijd worden de vruchten van het vorige jaar rijp. Deze struik is verwant an de rhododendron.

もがし科特有の小さなかん木でギリシャ中に見られ、ギリシャでは「クマラ」と呼ばれる。　見た目に美しいばかりでなく実は食用にも供される。　秋に開花すると同時に実をつける。

12. ARBUTUS UNEDO *L.*

This beautiful plant, with its flower-laden stems festooning the rocks, is one among the 50 species of Campanula found in Greece. Flowers April-June.

Diese schöne Pflanze, deren blühende Sprösse auf den Felsen kriechen, ist eine der 50 Arten von Campanula, die es in Griechenland gibt. Sie blüht im April-Juni.

Questa bella pianta i cui nuovi getti fioriti si arrampicano su per le rocce, è una delle cinquanta specie di campanelle esistenti in Grecia. Fiorisce in aprile-giugno.

Cette belle plante dont les nouveaux jets, pleins de fleurs, grimpent sur les rochers, est une des 50 espèces des clochettes qui se trouvent en Grèce. Elle fleurit en avril-juin.

Τό ὄμορφο αὐτό φυτό πού οἱ ὁλάνθιστοι βλαστοί του ἔρπουν ἐπάνω στούς βράχους εἶναι ἕνα ἀπό τά 50 εἴδη καμπανούλας πού ὑπάρχουν στήν Ἑλλάδα. Ἀνθίζει τόν Ἀπρίλιο- Ἰούνιο.

Denna underbara växt, vars nya skott fulla med små blommor kryper upp på klipporna, är en av de 50 sorterna, som finns i Grekland. Blommar i april-juni.

Deze fraaie plant, waarvan de rijkbloeiende twijgen over de rotsen kruipen, is een van de 50 in Griekenland voorkomende campanulasoorten. Bloeitijd april-juni.

岩肌を飾る茎もたわわな この美しい花は、ギリシャに見られる カンパヌラ 50品種のうちのひとつ。 開花期4～6月.

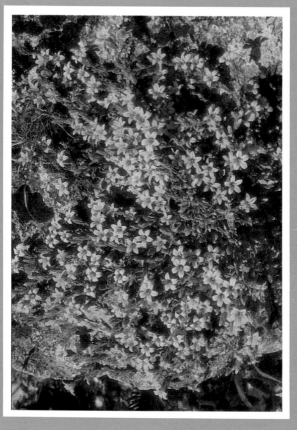

13. · **CAMPANULA RUPESTRIS** *SIBTH & SMITH*

This magnificent lily, with its intoxicating scent, grows on sandy shores throughout Greece. The development of the coastline in the interests of tourism has threatened this beautiful plant with extinction. It must be protected wherever it still exists. Flowers August-September.

Diese wundervolle Lilie mit ihrem berauschenden Duft lebt auf den sandigen Stränden ganz Griechenlands. Die touristische Verwertung der Küsten bedroht, diese schöne Pflanze total zu vernichten. Deshalb muss sie beschützt werden, wo immer sie noch zu finden ist. Sie blüht im August-September.

Questo superbo giglio dall'aroma inebriante cresce sulle coste sabbiose della Grecia. La valorizzazione turistica delle coste mette in pericolo la sopravvivenza di questa bella pianta. Per siffatta ragione la sua esistenza verrebbe preservata li dove ancora cresce. Fiorisce in agosto-settembre.

Ce superbe lis à l'arôme enivrant vit sur les côtes sablonneuses de la Grèce. La mise en valeur touristique de ces lieux menace la disparition totale de cette belle plante. Pour cette raison il est à conseiller de la protéger aux endroits où elle existe encore. Elle fleurit en août-septembre.

Ὁ ὑπέροχος αὐτός κρίνος μέ τό μεθυστικό ἄρωμα ζῆ στίς ἀμμώδεις παραλίες ὅλης τῆς Ἑλλάδος. Ἡ τουριστική ἀξιοποίηση τῶν ἀκτῶν ἀπειλεῖ τό ὡραῖο αὐτό φυτό μέ ὁλοκληρωτική ἐξαφάνιση. Γι' αὐτό πρέπει νά προστατεύεται ὅπου ὑπάρχει ἀκόμη. Ἀνθίζει τόν Αὔγουστο-Σεπτέμβριο.

Denna magnifika lilja med den bedövande doften, växer utefter sandiga stränder över hela Grekland. Då stränderna "värdesätts" ut turistsynpunkt, hotas denna växt av fullständig utrotning. Därför måste den skyddas, där den fortfarande växer. Blommar i augusti september.

Deze schitterend mooie lelie met zijn bedwelmende geur groeit op zandige kusten overal in Griekenland. De voorzieningen langs de kusten ten dienste van het toerisme bedreigen deze fraaie plant met uitroeiing. Daarom moet hij beschermd worden op die plaatsen waar hij nog voorkomt. Bloeitijd augustus-september.

魅惑的な香を漂わせるこの華麗な百合はギリシャ中の砂地に生えるが、今や、海岸線に浸透する観光の波が、この美しい植物を絶滅に追いやろうとしている。そんな中で、いまだに命を留めている所だけでもしっかりした保存を考える必要があろう。開花期8～9月.

14. PANCRATIUM MARITIMUM *L.*

With the advent of spring, low-lying brushwood and field become gay as they fill with anemones. The species illustrated is widely distributed and flowers from February to April.

Mit Einbruch des Frühlings werden alle buschigen Gegenden und Wiesen niedrigen Höhenmessers mit Anemonen voll. Eine sehr verbreitete Art ist auch die abgebildete Pflanze, die von Februar bis April blüht.

All'arrivo della primavera, le zone cespugliose ed i prati di bassa altitudine si coprono d'anemoni. Una specie diffusissima è quella illustrata che fiorisse in febbratio-aprile.

A l'arrivée du printemps, les lieux couverts de buissons et les prairies de basse altitude se remplissent d'anémones. Une espèce très répandue est celle de notre image qui fleurit en février-avril.

Μέ τόν ἐρχομό τῆς ἄνοιξης, οἱ θαμνότοποι καί τά λιβάδια χαμηλοῦ ὑψωμέτρου γεμίζουν μέ ἀνεμῶνες. Ένα πολύ διαδεδομένο εἶδος εἶναι καί τό εἰκονιζόμενο πού ἀνθίζει ἀπό τόν Φεβρουάριο ὡς τόν Ἀπρίλιο.

Då våren kommer, fylls buskvegetationen och ängar på låg höjd med anemoner. En mycket utbredd sort är den avbildade, som blommar från februari ända till april.

Bij het aanbreken van de lente staan alle laaggelegen gebieden met laag struikgewas en de weiden vol anemonen. Een zeer algemeen verbreide soort is de hier afgebeelde, die van februari tot april bloeit.

春の到来と共に　低地のかん木地帯や草地は、そこかしこで花を広けるアネモネで華やかな色あいを帯びてくる。　写真の品種は あまねく見られるもので、開花期は 2～4月.

15. **ANEMONE PAVONINA** *LAM.*
VAR. PURPUREO-VIOLACEA *BOISS.*

I his is one of the most attractive of the 25 species of the genus Colchicum to be found in Greece. It is endemic to Greek Macedonia and blooms in the autumn, producing first the large flower and then the leaves.

Ungefähr fünfundzwanzig Sorten der Gattung Colchicum leben in Griechenland. Eine der schönsten ist jene unserer Abbildung, welche ihre grossen Blüten im Herbst bekommt und zwar früher als ihre Blätter. Es ist eine endemische Pflanze aus griechisch-Mazedonien.

Sono all'incirca venticinque le specie del genere Colchium esistenti in Grecia. Una delle più belle è quella dell'illustrazione di cui i grandi fiori sbocciano prima delle foglie in autunno. È una pianta endemica della Macedonia ellenica.

Près de vingt cinq espèces du genre Colchicum vivent en Grèce. Une des plus belles est celle de notre image, dont les grandes fleurs s'épanouissent en automne avant ses feuilles. C'est une plante endémique de la Macédoine grecque.

Εικοσιπέντε περίπου εἴδη τοῦ γένους Colchicum ζουν στήν Ἑλλάδα. Ἕνα ἀπό τά ὡραιότερα εἶναι τό εἰκονιζόμενο πού τά μεγάλα ἄνθη του βγαίνουν τό φθινόπωρο πρίν ἀπό τά φύλλα. Εἶναι ἐνδημικό τῆς Ἑλληνικῆς Μακεδονίας.

Detta är en av de vackraste av de 25 sorterna av familjen Colchicum, som finns i Grekland. Den är inhemsk i grekiska Makedonien, och blommara på hösten, då först de stora blommorna kommer, innan bladen.

Ongeveer vijfentwintig soorten van het geslacht Colchicum komen voor in Griekenland. Een van de mooiste is de hier afgebeelde soort, die inheems is in Grieks Macedonië en die eerst zijn grote bloemen en daarna pas zijn bladeren vormt. Bloeitijd in de herfst.

ギリシャで見られる 25種もの同じ仲間の花々のうちでも、最も魅力的な品種のひとつでマケドニア特有。 葉が出るよりも早く、秋に大きな花を咲かせる。

16.   COLCHICUM BOWLESIANUM *B.L. BURT.*

This is a rare species endemic to Mount Taïyetos in the Peloponnese. It closely resembles G. nivalis, which is widely known in Europe, but differs chiefly in that it has an earlier, December, flowering and produces a flower before its leaves appear.

Seltene Pflanze endemisch auf dem Berge von Taigetos auf dem Peloponnes aufzufinden. Ähnelt sehr dem im übrigen Europa bekannten Galanthus Nivalis, unterscheidet sich aber hauptsächlich davon durch seine frühzeitige Blütezeit im Dezember und dadurch, dass seine Blüten früher erscheinen als seine Blätter.

Specie rara ed endemica del monte Taigeto del Peloponneso. Somiglia molto a quella nota in Europa sotto la denominazione di Galanthus Nivalis, con la differenza che i suoi fiori sbocciano prima delle foglie prematuramente in dicembre.

Espèce rare endémique du mont Taygète du Péloponnèse. Elle ressemble beaucoup à celle connue en Europe sous le nom de Galanthus Nivalis, mais elle diffère du fait que ses fleurs s'épanouissent avant ses feuilles et par sa floraison prématurée en décembre.

Σπάνιο εἶδος, ἐνδημικό τοῦ ὄρους Ταΰγετος τῆς Πελοποννήσου. Μοιάζει πολύ μέ τόν γνωστό στήν ὑπόλοιπη Εὐρώπη Galanthus Nivalis, διαφέρει ὅμως στήν πρώϊμη ἄνθηση τόν Δεκέμβριο καί στό ὅτι τά ἄνθη του βγαίνουν πρίν ἀπό τά φύλλα.

Sällsynt sort, inhemsk på Taygetosberget på Peloponnisos. Den liknar mycket den som är känd i Europa under namnet Galanthus Nivalis, men skiljer sig från den, huvudsakligen genom sin tidiga blomstring i december och att blomman skjuter upp, innan bladen kommer.

Een zeldzame plant, inheems op de berg Taÿgetos op de Peloponnesus. Hij lijkt sterk op de in het overige deel van Europa bekende Galanthus Nivalis (sneeuwklokje), maar verschilt daarvan voornamelijk door zijn vroege bloei in december en door het feit dat de bloemen eerder verschijnen dan de bladeren.

ペロポネソスの タイエトス山 特有の珍種. ヨーロッパで広く知られる G. ニバリスによく似ているが. 12月にはもう葉が出る前に花をつける点が異なる.

17. GALANTHUS REGINAE OLGAE *ORPH.*

Common plant found almost everywhere in Greece. It grows in bushy areas and, at low altitudes, in woods. Flowers February-April.

Eine gewöhnliche Pflanze in ganz Griechenland. Lebt an buschigen Stellen und in Wäldern niedrigen Höhenmessers. Blüht im Ferbuar-April.

Pianta comune che cresce quasi in tutta la Grecia. Cresce nelle zone cespugliose e nei boschi di bassa altitudine. Fiorisce in febbraio-aprile.

Plante commune presque dans toute la Grèce. Elle crôt dans les lieux buissonneux et les bois de basse altitude. Elle fleurit en février-avril.

Φυτό κοινό σ' όλη σχεδόν τήν Ελλάδα. Ζῆ στούς θαμνότοπους καί τά δάση χαμηλού ὑψομέτρου. Ἀνθίζει τόν Φεβρουάριο-Ἀπρίλιο.

En vanlig växt i nästan hela Grekland. Växer på buskiga platser och i skogar på låg höjd. Blommar i februari-april.

Een bijna overal in Griekenland algemeen voorkomende plant, die in streken met struikgewas en in bossen op geringe hoogte groeit. Bloeitijd februari - april.

ギリシャ全土ほとんどどこにでも見られる一般的な花. かく木地帯や森の低地の部分に咲く. 開花期2～4月.

18. **ARISARUM VULGARE** *TARG.*

A lovely species which grows in mountain meadows.
It is widely distributed on the mainland as well as on
those islands which boast high mountains. Flowers
April-May.

Eine hübsche Art Tulpe, die auf den Wiesen der
gebirgigen Zone lebt. Ziemlich stark verbreitet
sowohl auf dem Festland als auch auf den Inseln, die
hohe Berge haben. Blüht im April-Mai.

Bella specie di tulipano che cresce nei prati delle
zone montuose. E'assai diffusa sia nella Grecia
continentale che nelle isole coperte di alte montagne.
Fiorisce in aprile-maggio.

C'est une belle espèce de tulipe qui vit dans les
prairies de la zone montagneuse. Elle est assez
répandue tant en Grèce continentale qu'aux îles aux
grandes montagnes. Elle fleurit en avril-mai.

῍Ομορφο εἶδος τουλίπας πού ζῆ στά λιβάδια τῆς ὀρεινῆς
ζώνης. Εἶναι ἀρκετά διαδεδομένο τόσο στήν ἠπειρωτική
᾿Ελλάδα ὅσο καί στά νησιά πού ἔχουν μεγάλα βουνα.
᾿Ανθίζει τόν ᾿Απρίλιο-Μάϊο.

En vacker sort av tulpan-familjen, som växer på
ängarna i bergszonen. Den är tämligen utbredd både
på grekiska fastlandet och på öarna, som har höga
berg. Blommar i april-maj.

Een fraaie soort tulp van de bergweiden, die vrij
algemeen voorkomt op het Griekse vasteland en op
die eilanden die hoge bergen hebben. Bloeitijd april-
mei.

山の草地に咲く愛らしい花．ギリシャ本土，並びに高山の
ある島々に見られる．　開花期4〜5月．

19. **TULIPA HAGERI** *HELDR.*

The most common of the 6 species of Cyclamen to be found in Greece. It has heart-shaped leaves and a large, globular corm. Flowers September-November.

Die gewöhnlichste unter den 6 Arten von Zyclamen, die in Griechenland leben. Hat eine grosse und kugelförmige Zwiebel, und die Blätter haben die Form des Herzens. Blüht im September-November.

E'la più comune delle sei specie di ciclamini esistenti in Grecia. Si presenta come un gran bulbo sferico e le sue foglie sono a forma di cuore. Fiorisce in settembre-novembre.

C'est la plus commune des six espèces du cyclamen qui vivent en Grèce. Elle forme un grand bulbe arrondi et ses feuilles ont la forme de coeur. Elle donne ses fleurs en septembre-novembre.

Τό πιό κοινό ἀπό τά 6 εἴδη κυκλάμινου πού ζοῦν στήν Ἑλλάδα. Κάνει βολβό μεγάλο, σφαιρικό καί φύλλα καρδιοειδῆ. Ἀνθίζει τόν Σεπτέμβριο-Νοέμβριο.

Den vanligaste av de sex slags cyklamen, som växer i Grekland. Den har en stor, rund lök och hjärtformade blad. Blommar i september-november.

De gewoonste van de 6 soorten Cyclamen die in Griekenland voorkomen. De knol is groot en rond, en de bladeren zijn hartvormig. Bloeitijd september-november.

ギリシャで見られる6種のシクラメンのうちでも最も一般的なもの。ハート型の葉と大きな球茎を持つ。　開花期9～11月

20. **CYCLAMEN GRAECUM** *LAM.*

A lovely species of wild violet common to the mountains of the mainland, including the Peloponnese. Flowers May-July.

Schöne Sorte des wilden Veilchens, sehr gewöhnlich auf den Bergen des kontinentalen Griechenlands und des Peloponnes. Blüht im Mai-Juli.

Specie di viola selvatica diffusissima su per i monti della Grecia continentale e del Peloponneso. Fiorisce in maggio-luglio.

Espèce de violette sauvage très connue dans les montagnes de la Grèce continentale et du Péloponnèse. Elle fleurit en mai-juillet.

Όμορφο είδος άγιομενεξέ κοινό στά βουνά τής ήπειρωτικής Ελλάδος καί τής Πελοποννήσου. Ανθίζει τόν Μάϊο- Ιούλιο.

En vacker sort av vildvioletter vanlig i bergen på grekiska fastlandet och på Peloponnisos. Blommar i maj-juli.

Een fraaie soort wild viooltje, zeer algemeen in de bergen op het Griekse vasteland en de Peloponnesus. Bloeitijd mei-juli.

ペロポネソスを含むギリシャ本土に一般に見られる愛らしい野生のスミレ。　開花期 5~7月.

21. VIOLA TRICOLOR *L.*
SSP. MACEDONICA *(BOISS. & HELDR.) A. SCHMIDT*

This species is common to the mountains of Europe but rare in Greece. It may be found on Mount Olympus and in the Pindus Range. It is called "the mountain climbers' barometer" because its petals close in response to increased humidity in the atmosphere. Flowers August-September.

Sehr gewöhnlich auf Bergen in Europa, aber sehr selten in Griechenland zu finden. Man trifft es auf dem Olymp und auf dem Gebirge von Pindos. Es wird das Barometer der Bergsteiger genannt, weil seine Blüten sogleich schliessen, wenn die Atmosphäre feucht zu beginnen wird. Es blüht im August-September.

Specie comunissima nelle regioni montuose d'Europa, tuttavia rarissima in Grecia. Cresce sull' Olimpo e sulla catena montuosa del Pindos. Siffatta specie viene chiamata «barometro dei montanari» poiché i suoi fiori si rinchiudono non appena l'atmosfera comincia a farsi umida. Fiorisce in agosto-settembre.

Espèce commune dans les montagnes de l'Europe mais rare en Grèce. On la rencontre dans l'Olympe et la châne montagneuse de Pindos. On l'appelle «baromètre des montagnards» parce que ses fleurs se referment subitement lorsque l'atmosphère commence à devenir humide. Elle fleurit en août-septembre.

Εἶδος κοινό στά βουνά τῆς Εὐρώπης ἀλλά σπάνιο στήν Ἑλλάδα. Ἀπαντᾶται στόν Ὄλυμπο καί στήν ὁροσειρά τῆς Πίνδου. Λέγεται τό βαρόμετρο τῶν ὀρειβατῶν γιατί τά ἄνθη του κλείνουν ἀμέσως μόλις ἡ ἀτμόσφαιρα ἀρχίζει νά γίνεται ὑγρή. Ἀνθίζει τόν Αὔγουστο-Σεπτέμβριο.

Denna sort är vanlig på bergen i Europa, men ovanlig i Grekland. Man möter den på Olympos (Olympen) och på Pindosbergskedjan. Den kallas för bergsklättrarnas barometer, därför att dess blommor fäller ihop sig, så snart atmosfären blir fuktig. Blommar i augusti-september.

Zeer algemeen in de bergen van Europa, maar zeldzaam in Griekenland, waar hij voorkomt op de berg Olympus en op de bergketen van de Pindus. Hij wordt de "barometer van de bergbeklimmers" genoemd, omdat zijn bloemen zich sluiten zodra de atmosfeer vochtig begint te worden. Bloeitijd augustus-september.

この品種はヨーロッパの山々によく見られるが、ギリシャでは珍しく、オリンパス山とピンドウス山脈に咲く。 湿度が上がると花びらを閉じるため、「登山者のバロメーター」とも呼ばれる。開花期 8〜9月.

22.   CARLINA ACAULIS *L.* VAR. ALPINA *JACQ.*

This is surely one of the most beautiful of Greek wild flowers. It is an endemic and is found in mountain forests from western Macedonia to the Peloponnese. Flowers June-August.

Dies ist eine der schönsten griechischen Wildpflanzen. Eine endemische Pflanze Griechenlands, die in den Wäldern der Berge von West-Mazedonien bis zum Peloponnes lebt. Blüht im Juni-August.

Questa pianta è uno dei più bei fiori selvatici della Grecia. Trattasi di una pianta endemica dei boschi delle montagne della Macedonia occidentale fino a quelli del Peloponneso. Fiorisce in luglio-agosto.

Cette plante est une des plus belles fleurs sauvages de la Grèce. Elle est endémique des bois des montagnes de la Macédoine occidentale jusqu'à ceux du Péloponnése. Elle donne ses fleurs en juin-août.

Τό φυτό αὐτό εἶναι ἕνα ἀπό τά ὡραιότερα ἑλληνικά ἀγριολούλουδα. Εἶναι ἐνδημικό καί ζῆ στά δάση τῶν βουνῶν ἀπό τήν Δ. Μακεδονία ὡς τήν Πελοπόννησο. Ἀνθίζει τόν Ἰούνιο-Αὔγουστο.

Denna växt är en av de vackraste vildblommorna i Grekland. Den är inhemsk i Grekland och växer i bergsskogarna från västra Makedonien till Peloponnisos. Blommar i juni-augusti.

Een van de mooiste Griekse wilde bloemen, die inheems is in de bergwouden van West-Macedonië tot de Peloponnesus. Bloeitijd juni-augustus.

ギリシャの野生の花々のうちでも大へん美しいもの。西部マケドニアからペロポネソスにかけての山々の森に咲く。 開花期 6〜8月.

23.   LILIUM CHALCEDONICUM *L.*

This species is endemic to Greece. It grows in mountain meadows as well as in low-lying bushy areas. Flowers November-January.

Endemische Pflanze Griechenlands, die von November bis Januar blüht. Lebt auf Wiesen gebirgiger Zone aber auch an buschbewachsenen Stellen niedrigen Höhenmessers.

Specie endemica della Grecia che fiorisce in novembre-gennaio. Cresce nei prati delle zone montuose, nonché nelle regioni cespugliose di bassa altitudine.

C'est une espèce qui vit en Grèce et fleurit en novembre-janvier. Elle pousse dans les prairies de la zone montagneuse, ainsi que dans les lieux buissonneux de basse altitude.

Εἶδος ἐνδημικό τῆς Ἑλλάδος πού ἀνθίζει τόν Νοέμβριο-Ἰανουάριο. Ζῆ σέ λιβάδια τῆς ὀρεινῆς ζώνης ἀλλά καί σέ θαμνότοπους χαμηλοῦ ὑψομέτρου.

En inhemsk krokus i Grekland, som blommar ifrån november till januari. Växer på ängar i bergszonen, men också på platser med buskar på låg höjd.

Een in Griekenland inheemse crocussoort, die van november tot januari bloeit. Hij groeit zowel op bergweiden als in laag gelegen streken met struikgewas.

ギリシャ特有の花で, 山あいの草地と低地のかん木地帯に咲く. 開花期 11～1月.

24. CROCUS LAEVIGATUS *BORY & CHAUBARD*

This extremely rare species of campanula is endemic to Greece. It grows among the rocks of the mountains of Central Greece. Flowers June-September.

Eine sehr seltene Campanula, endemisch, auf den Felsen der hohen Berge in Mittelgriechenland zu finden. Ihre Blüten erscheinen von Juni-bis September

Specie rarissima di campanella endemica delle rocce alpine delle montagne della Grecia centrale. I suoi fiori sbocciano in giugno-settembre.

Espèce très rare de clochette endémique des roches alpins des montagnes de la Grèce centrale. Ses fleurs paraissent en juin-septembre.

Πολύ σπάνιο είδος καμπανούλας ένδημικό τῶν άλπικῶν βράχων τῶν βουνῶν τῆς Κεντρικῆς Έλλάδος. Τά ἄνθη της κάνουν τήν ἐμφάνισή τους ἀπό τόν Ἰούνιο ὡς τόν Σεπτέμβριο.

Denna ytterst ovanliga sort bland Klockorna är inhemsk bland fjällklippor på centrala Greklandsberg. Blommorna skjuter upp från juni-september.

Deze zeer zeldzame campanula-soort is inheems in het hoge bergland van Centraal Griekenland, waar hij tussen de rotsen groeit. Bloeitijd juni-september.

キリシャ特有の非常に珍しい品種. 中部キリシャの山々の岩間に咲く高山植物. 開花期 6〜9月.

25. **CAMPANULA RUPICOLA** *BOISS. & SPRUN.*

This species is one of the multitude of wild violets which grow in Greece. It is found in the Pindus Range. Flowers July-August.

Diese Art ist eine der vielen Wildveilchen, die in Griechenland leben. Wächst auf dem Gebirge von Pindos und blüht im Juli-August.

Questa specie è una delle numerose mammole selvatiche che crescono in Grecia. Spunta su per la catena montuosa del monte Pindos e fiorisce in luglio-agosto.

Cette espèce est une des plusieurs violettes sauvages qui croissent en Grèce. Elle pousse dans la chäne montagneuse du mont Pindos et elle fleurit en juillet-aout.

Τό είδος αὐτό εἶναι ἕνας ἀπό τούς πολλούς ἀγριο-μενεξέδες πού ζοῦν στήν Ἑλλάδα. Φυτρώνει στήν ὁροσειρά τῆς Πίνδου καί ἀνθίζει τόν Ἰούλιο-Αὔγουστο.

En sorts vildviolett, av de många som växer i Grekland. Skjuter upp på Pindos-bergskedjan och blommar i juli-augusti.

Een van de vele soorten wilde viooltjes die in Griekenland voorkomen. Deze soort groeit op de beraketens van de Pindus en bloeit in juli-augustus.

ギリシャに咲く多数の野生のスミレのひとつで. ピンドウス山脈に見られる.　開花期 7〜8月.

26. **VIOLA MAGELLENSIS** *PORTA & RIGO.*

A cosmopolitan plant grows in South America and
the Mediterranean. In Greece it is found on sandy
shores in Rhodes and the Peloponnese. Flowers in
the Autumn.

Eine kosmopolitische Pflanze, die an vielen Stellen
aufgefunden worden ist vom Mittelmeer bis Süda-
merika. Lebt auf sandigen Stränden und blüht im
Herbst. In Griechenland ist es aus Rhodos und dem
Süd-Peloponnes bekannt.

Pianta cosmopolita che cresce in numerose regioni,
nelle regioni mediterranee come nell'America del
Sud. Spunta nelle zone sabbiose delle coste in
autunno. In Grecia cresce nell'isola di Rodi e nel Sud
del Peloponneso.

Plante cosmopolite qui se trouve dans plusieurs
étendues, depuis la Méditerranée jusqu'en Amérique
du Sud. Elle crôt dans les côtes sablonneuses et
fleurit en automne. En Grèce elle est connue à l'île de
Rhodes et dans le Sud du Péloponnèse.

Φυτό κοσμοπολιτικό πού ἔχει βρεθεῖ σέ πολλές
περιοχές ἀπό τήν Μεσόγειο ὥς τήν Ν. ᾿Αμερική. Στήν
῾Ελλάδα εἶναι γνωστό ἀπό τήν Ρόδο καί τήν Ν.
Πελοπόννησο. Ζῆ στίς ἀμμώδεις παραλίες καί ἀνθίζει τό
φθινόπωρο.

En kosmopolitisk växt, som man funnit i många
trakter ifrån Medelhavet ända till Sydafrika. I
Grekland finner man den på Rhodos och södra
Peloponnisos. Växer på sandstränder och blommar
på hösten.

Een cosmopolitische plant, die in tal van streken
langs de Middellandse Zee tot in Zuid-Amerika
voorkomt. In Griekenland is hij bekend op Rhodos en
in het Zuiden van de Peloponnesus. Hij groeit op
zandstranden en bloeit in de herfst.

南アメリカから 地中海のどこにもある花のコスモポリタン。
ギリシャでは ロードス島と ペロポネソスの砂地に 咲く。　開
花期は 秋。

27. IPOMOEA STOLONIFERA *(CYRILLO)* *G.F. GMELIN*

This charming plant grows in the mountain forests of northern and central Greece. Flowers June-August.

Diese niedliche Pflanze lebt in den Wäldern der Berge in Nord - und Mittelgriechenland. Blüht im Juni-August.

Questa pianta affascinante cresce nei boschi delle montagne della Grecia centrale e settentrionale. Fiorisce in giugno-agosto.

Cette charmante. plante pousse dans les bois des montagnes de la Grèce centrale et du Nord. Elle donne ses fleurs en juin-août.

Τό χαριτωμένο αὐτό φυτό ζῆ μέσα στά δάση τῶν βουνῶν στήν Βόρεια καί Κεντρική Ἑλλάδα. Ἀνθίζει τόν Ἰούνιο-Αὔγουστο.

Denna söta växt finner man i skogarna på bergen i norra och centrala Grekland. Blommar i juni-augusti.

Deze sierlijke plant groeit in de bergwouden in Noord- en Centraal Griekenland. Bloeitijd juni-augustus.

北部並びに 中部ギリシャの山々の森に咲くチャーミングな花.
開花期 6〜8月 .

28. CORONILLA VARIA L.

Common to southern Greece, this plant favours sandy places and low-lying fallow grounds. Flowers April-June.

Gewöhnliche Pflanze aus Süd-Griechenland, die Strandorte und unkultiviertes Land bevorzugt, die einen niedrigen Höhenmesser haben. Blüht im April-Juni.

Pianta comune in Grecia meridionale che preferisce le coste e le zone incolte di bassa altitudine. Fiorisce in aprile-giugno.

Plante commune en Grèce du Sud qui préfère vivre près des côtes et dans les lieux incultes de basse altitude. Elle fleurit en avril-juin.

Φυτό κοινό στήν Ν. 'Ελλάδα πού προτιμᾶ τίς παραλιακές τοποθεσίες καί τούς χέρσους τόπους χαμηλοῦ ὑψομέτρου. 'Ανθίζει τόν 'Απρίλιο-'Ιούνιο.

En vanlig växt i södra Grekland, där den föredrar platser nära havet och obrukade marker på låg höjd. Blommar i april-juni.

Een in Zuid-Griekenland algemeen voorkomende plant, die bij voorkeur aan de kust en op laaggelegen woeste gronden groeit. Bloeitijd april-juni.

南ギリシャによく見られ. 砂地や低地の休耕地を好む.
開花期 4～6月.

29. **RESEDA ALBA** *L.*

This dward iris is widely distributed throughout southern Greece and the islands of the Aegean. Its colours vary from deep violet to white and yellow. Flowers March-May.

Kleine Lilie sehr bekannt in ganz Süd-Griechenland und auf den Inseln des Ägaäischen Meeres. Ihre Farbe variiert zwischen dunkel violett und weiss oder gelb. Sie blüht im März-Mai.

Piccolo giglio diffuso in tutta la Grecia meridionale e nelle isole dell'Egeo. Il suo colore varia dal viola scuro al bianco ed al giallo. Fiorisce in marzo-maggio.

Petit lis très répandu dans toute la Grèce du Sud et dans les îles de la mer Egée. Sa couleur varie du violet foncé au blanc et au jaune. Il fleurit en mars-mai.

Μικρό κρινάκι πολύ διαδεδομένο σ' ὅλη τήν ῾Ελλάδα καί τά νησιά τοῦ Αἰγαίου. Τό χρῶμα του ποικίλλει ἀπό τό βαθύ ἰῶδες ὥς τό λευκό καί τό κίτρινο. ᾽Ανθίζει τόν Μάρτιο-Μάιο.

En liten lilja, mycket utbredd i hela Sydgrekland och öarna i det Egeiska havet. Färgen skiftar ifrån mörk jod till vit och gul. Blommar i mars-maj.

Deze dwerg-iris is zeer algemeen in heel Zuid-Griekenland en op de eilanden in de Egeïsche Zee. De kleur varieert van donkerpaars tot wit en geel. Bloeitijd maart-mei.

この小さなアイリスは、特に南ギリシャとエーゲ海の島々によく見られる。 濃い紫色から白、黄色と様々の色の花を咲かせる。 開花期 3～5月.

30. **IRIS PUMILA** *L.* **VAR. ATTICA** *BOISS. & HELDR.*

This common member of the Greek flora is found in low-lying fields and bushy places. Its flowers, known to pharmacologists as "Flores Malvae," are used in a folk remedy for throat and stomach ailments.

Eine gewöhnliche Abart der griechischen Flora. Sie lebt auf Feldern und an buschigen Stellen niedrigen Höhenmesses. Ihre Blüten - bekannt bei den Apothekern als Flores Malvae - werden von den Leuten als Linderungsmittel für Hals und Magen gebraucht. Sie blüht im Frühling.

Specie comune della flora greca. Cresce nei campi e nelle zone cespugliose di bassa altitudine. I suoi fiori noti ai farmacisti come Flores Malvae, vengono utilizzati dal popolo per ammorbire il mal di gola ed i dolori stomacali. Fiorisce in primavera.

Espèce commune de la flore grecque. Elle vit dans les champs et dans les lieux buissonneux de basse altitude. Ses fleurs connues aux pharmaciens comme Flores Malvae, sont utilisées par le peuple comme adoucissant pour la gorge et l'estomac. Elle fleurit au printemps.

Εἶδος κοινό τῆς ἑλληνικῆς χλωρίδος. Ζῆ στά χωράφια καί στούς θαμνότοπους χαμηλοῦ ὑψομέτρου. Τά ἄνθη του, γνωστά στούς φαρμακοποιούς σάν Flores malvae χρησιμοποιοῦνται ἀπό τόν λαό σάν μαλακτικά γιά τόν λαιμό καί τό στομάχι. Ἀνθίζει τήν ἄνοιξη.

En vanlig växt i den grekiska floran. Växer på åkrar och i buskvegetation på låg höjd. Dess blommor, kända bland apotekare som Flores Malvae, används allmänt som skonande mot hals- och magont. Blommar på våren.

Een algemeen voorkomend lid van de Griekse flora, dat groeit op weiden en op laaggelegen, met struikgewas begroeide gronden. De bloemen - bij de apothekers bekend als "flores Malvae" - worden door de bevolking gebruikt als geneesmiddel tegen keel-en maagaandoeningen. Bloeitijd in de lente.

ギリシャでは大へん一般的な花で、低地の草原やかん木地帯を好む。 薬草学者には「フロレス マルバエ」として知られ、のどやお腹の薬として用いられている。

31. MALVA SILVESTRIS *L.*

This plant is commonly seen on the hillsides of southern Greece and in the islands. Its colours range from white to violet traversed with dark veins. Flowers September-October.

Gewöhnliche Pflanze der niedrigen Hügel Süd-griechenlands und der Inseln. Ihre Blüten variieren zwischen weiss und violett und werden durch dunkle Nervaturen durchlaufen. Sie blüht im September-Oktober.

Pianta comune che cresce su per le basse colline della Grecia meridionale e nelle isole. I suoi fiori variano dal bianco al viola con venature scure. I suoi fiori sbocciano in settembre-ottobre.

Plante commune vivant dans les basses collines de la Grèce du Sud et dans les îles. Ses fleurs varient du blanc au violet et sont traversées par des nervures de couleur foncée. Elle donne ses fleurs en septembre-octobre.

Φυτό κοινό στούς χαμηλούς λόφους τῆς Ν. ΄Ελλάδος καί τῶν νησιῶν. Τά ἄνθη του ποικίλλουν ἀπό τό λευκό μέχρι τό ἰῶδες καί διατρέχονται ἀπό σκοῦρες νευρώσεις. ΄Ανθίζει τόν Σεπτέμβριο-΄Οκτώβριο.

En vanlig växt på låga kullar i södra Grekland och på öarna. Blommorna skiftar från vitt till lila och har mörka nervränder. Blommar september-oktober.

Een op lage heuvels in Zuid-Griekenland en op de Griekse eilanden algemeen voorkomende plant. De bloemen variëren van wit tot lila en hebben donkergekleurde nerfstrepen. Bloeitȳd september-oktober.

南部ギリシャと島々の丘陵地帯に見られる。色は白から、濃いしきのはいった紫と様々である。 開花期9～10月.

32.   CROCUS PALLASII *M. B.*
VAR. CARTWRIGHTIANUS *HERB.*

This species of anemone, found throughout Greece, is the progenitor of the cultivated varieties. Its coloration is highly varied, and may be white, rose, purple, red or blue. It grows in fields and meadows at low altitude. Flowers February-April.

Diese Abart von Anemone, gewöhnlich in ganz Griechenland, ist der Vorgänger der aufgezogenen Variationen. Wir treffen sie in verschiedenen Farbtönen von weiss und rosig bis sauerkirschrot, rot und hellblau. Sie lebt auf Feldern und Wiesen niedrigen Höhenmessers. Sie blüht im Februar-April.

Questa specie d'anemone comune è l'antenato delle varietà coltivate. Si trova in diverse sfumature, dal bianco e rosa allo scarlatto e azzurro. Cresce nei campi e nei prati di bassa altitudine. Fiorisce in febbraio-aprile.

Cette espèce d'anémone commune dans toute la Grèce est l'ancêtre des variétés cultivées. Nous la rencontrons en diverses nuances, du blanc et rose au cramoisi rouge et bleu ciel. Elle croît dans les champs et prairies de basse altitude. Elle fleurit en février-avril.

Τό εἶδος αὐτό ἀνεμώνας, κοινό σ' ὅλη τήν Ἑλλάδα, εἶναι ὁ πρόγονος τῶν καλλιεργουμένων ποικιλιῶν. Τό συναντοῦμε σέ διάφορες ἀποχρώσεις ἀπό τό λευκό καί τό ρόδινο ὥς τό βυσσινί, τό κόκκινο καί τό γαλάζιο. Ζῆ στά χωράφια καί τά λιβάδια χαμηλοῦ ὑψομέτρου. Ἀνθίζει τόν Φεβρουάριο-Ἀπρίλιο.

Denna sorts anemon, som är vanlig i hela Grekland, är förfadern till de odlade sorterna. Man möter den i olika skiftningar från vitt och rosa till mörk-lila, rött och blått. Växer på åkrarna och ängarna på låg höjd. Blommar i februari-april.

Deze in heel Griekenland algemene soort anemoon is de voorouder van alle gekweekte variëteiten. Men vindt ze in verschillende kleuren van wit en lichtrose tot donkerrood, rood en hemelsblauw. Hij groeit op laaggelegen velden en weiden. Bloeitijd februari-april.

ギリシャ中で目につくこのアネモネは、栽培品種の原本である。色は白、バラ色、紫、赤、青と様々である。 低地の草原を好む。 開花期 2～4月。

33.   ANEMONE CORONARIA *L.*

Met in abundance in southern Greece and on the Aegean and Ionian islands, this maritime species gives off a wonderful perfume, especially at evening. Flowers February-April.

Gewöhnliche Abart aus Süd - Griechenland, den Inseln des Ägaischen und Ionischen Meeres. Sie lebt an Stellen nahe am Meere gelegen und blüht im Februar-April. Ihre Blüten sprühen ein wunderschönes Aroma abends aus.

Specie comune in Grecia meridionale come pure nelle isole dell'Egeo e dell'Ionio. Cresce nelle vicinanze del mare e fiorisce in febbraio-aprile. I suoi fiori esalano di notte un aroma superbo.

Espèce commune en Grèce du Sud ainsi que dans les îles de la mer Egée et de la mer Ionienne. Elle cröt près de la mer et elle fleurit en février-avril. Ses fleurs exhalent pendant la nuit un arôme superbe.

Είδος κοινό στήν Ν. ΄Ελλάδα καί τά νησιά τοῦ Αἰγαίου καί τοῦ ᾽Ιονίου. Ζῆ σέ παραθαλάσσιες τοποθεσίες καί ἀνθίζει τόν Φεβρουάριο-᾽Απρίλιο. Τά ἄνθη του ἀναδίνουν τό βράδυ ἕνα θαυμάσιο ἄρωμα.

Finns i överflöd i Södra Grekland och på de egeiska och joniska öarna. Växer på platser nära havet och blommar i februari-april. Blommorna sprider på kvällen en underbar doft.

Een in Zuid-Griekenland en op de Ege sche en de Ionische eilanden algemeen voorkomende plant, die dicht bij zee groeit en in februari-april bloeit. De bloemen verspreiden 's nachts een heerlijke geur.

海岸に近く咲き，南ギリシャとエーゲ，イオニア海の島々に豊富に見られる． 夕方になると素晴しい香を漂わせる． 開花期2～4月．

34.   **MATHIOLA SINUATA** *R. BR.*

This charming little plant grows in sub-alpine woodlands throughout most of the mainland. Its flowers may de deep violet, white or rose. Flowers April-June.

Diese niedliche Pflanze lebt in Wäldern auf den Bergen fast im ganzen festländischen Griechenland. Die Farbe ihrer Blumen variiert zwischen dunkel violett und weiss oder rosa. Sie blüht im April-Juni.

Questa pianta cos' bellina spunta nei boschi delle montagne di tutta la Grecia continentale. Il colore dei suoi fiori varia dal viola scuro al bianco ed al rosa. Fiorisce in aprile-giugno.

Cette plante charmante pousse dans les bois des montagnes de toute la Grèce continentale. La couleur de ses fleurs varie du violet foncé au blanc et au rose. Elle fleurit en avril-juin.

Αὐτό τό χαριτωμένο φυτό ζῆ στά δάση τῶν βουνῶν σ' ὁλόκληρη σχεδόν τήν ἠπειρωτική Ἑλλάδα. Τό χρῶμα τῶν λουλουδιῶν του ποικίλλει ἀπό τό βαθύ ἰῶδες ὥς τό λευκό καί τό ρόδινο. Ἀνθίζει τόν Ἀπρίλιο- Ἰούνιο.

Denna söta planta finner man i bergsskogarna i nästan hela Greklands fastland. Blommornas färg varierar från mörk röd till vit och rosa. Blommar i april-juni.

Dit aardige plantje groeit in debergbossen in bijna heel Centraal Griekenland. De kleur van de bloemen varieert van donkerpaars tot wit en rose. Bloeitijd april-juni.

ギリシャ本土のやや高地の森林地帯に見られる かわいらしい 花. 濃い紫, 白, ピンクと様々な色がある. 開花期4〜 6月.

35.   **ANEMONE BLANDA** *SCHOTT & KOTSCHI*

This wonderful iris with its sparkling white flowers is cultivated all over Greece. It is also a native and is widely encountered growing in the wild. Flowers March-April.

Diese wunderschöne Lilie mit ihren schneeweissen Blüten wird in ganz Griechenland aufgezogen. An vielen Orten trifft man sie auch wildwachsend. Sie blüht im März-April.

Questo splendido giglio di fiori bianchi viene coltivato in Grecia. In numerose regioni cresce da sé. Fiorisce in marzo-aprile.

Ce lis splendide aux fleurs blanches se cultive partout en Grèce. Dans plusieurs endroits il crôt tout seul. Il fleurit en mars-avril.

Ο θαυμάσιος αὐτός κρίνος μέ τά κατάλευκα ἄνθη καλλιεργεῖται σ' ὅλη τήν Ἑλλάδα. Σέ πολλές περιοχές τόν βρίσκουμε αὐτοφυή. Ἀνθίζει τόν Μάρτιο-Ἀπρίλιο.

Denna underbara lilja med de helt vita blommorna odlas i hela Grekland. I många trakter finns den även i vilt tillstånd. Blommar mars-april.

Deze schitterende lelie met zijn spierwitte bloemen wordt overal in Griekenland gekweekt. Op vele plaatsen groeit hij ook in het wild Bloeitijd maart-april.

まぶしいばかりに白い、この素晴しいアイリスは ギリシャ全土で栽培されているが、野生のものも広く見つけることができる。 開花期3～4月.

36. IRIS FLORENTINA *L.*

More than 40 species and subspecies of the genus
Viola are found in Greece. One is the captivating V.
Dukadjinica which grows on Mount Smolika and
neighbouring peaks near the mountains of Albania.
Flowers July-August.

Mehr als 40 Abarten und Untersorten der Gattung
Viola leben im griechischen Raum. Eine davon ist
auch die reizende Viola Dukadjinica, die auf dem
Berg Smolikas und auf anderen benachbarten
Bergen Albaniens wächst. Sie blüht im Juli-August.

Più di quaranta specie e sottospecie del genere Viola
si possono incontrare in Grecia. Una è la bella Viola
Ducadjinica che cresce su per la montagna Smolikas
e in altre montagne presso l'Albania. Fiorisce in
luglio-agosto.

Plus de quarante espèces et sous-espèces du genre
Viola peuvent se rencontrer en Grèce. Une d'elles est
la charmante Viola Ducadjinica qui crôt dans la
montagne Smolikas et dans d'autres montagnes près
de l'Albanie. Elle donne ses fleurs en juillet-aout.

Περισσότερα ἀπό 40 εἴδη καί ὑποείδη τοῦ γένους Viola
ζοῦν στόν ἑλληνικό χώρο. Ἕνα ἀπό αὐτά εἶναι ἡ
χαριτωμένη Viola Dukadjinica πού φυτρώνει στό ὄρος
Σμόλικας καί ἄλλα γειτονικά μέ τήν Ἀλβανία βουνά.
Ἀνθίζει τόν Ἰούλιο-Αὔγουστο.

Det växer mer än 40 sorter och undersorter av
familjen Viola i Grekland. En av dem är den söta Viola
Dukadjinica som skjuter upp på Smolikas-berget och
andra berg i närheten av Albanien. Blommar i juli-
augusti.

Meer dan 40 variëteiten en sub-variëteiten van het
geslacht Viola komen in Griekenland voor. Een
daarvan is de aantrekkelijke Viola dukadjinica, die op
de berg Smolikas en op andere bergen bij Albanië
groeit. Bloeitijd juli-augustus.

ギリシャにある40以上もの同品種の花々のうちでも これは
非常に魅力的な品種． スモリカ山と アルバニアの山々の
近くに咲く． 開花期7〜8月．

37. **VIOLA DUKADJINICA** *W. BECKER & KOSANIN*